The Way of the Dragon

by
China Smith

Sarasota, Florida

Joseph Anthony Schroeder
CONTRIBUTING EDITOR

Copyright © China Smith, 2019

All rights reserved. Published by the Peppertree Press, LLC.
The Peppertree Press and associated logos are trademarks of
the Peppertree Press, LLC.

No part of this publication may be reproduced, stored in a retrieval system, transmitted in any form or by any means, electronic, mechanical, photocopying, recording, or otherwise, without prior written permission of the publisher and author/illustrator.
Graphic design by Rebecca Barbier.

For information regarding permission,
call 941-922-2662 or contact us at our website:
www.peppertreepublishing.com or write to:
the Peppertree Press, LLC.
Attention: Publisher
1269 First Street, Suite 7
Sarasota, Florida 34236

ISBN: 978-1-61493-657-2

Library of Congress Number: 2019942066

Printed June 2019

I dedicate this book to my creator, God and to my Dad, China Smith Sr. and my Mom, Victoria Pompey Parker. Thank you for giving me life! I pray that I have made you proud of who I have become, and what I have accomplished. The best is yet to come! Hold on!

My Heartfelt Thanks

I want thank and honor my God, the Lord Jesus Christ and the Holy Spirit, I give Him all the glory and praise!

Thank you Mom, Victoria Pompey Parker and my Dad, China Smith, Sr. for giving me life and loving me unconditionally.

Thank you to each of my three beautiful kids, Briauna, China III and my little mascot, Estella and also to their mother. Thank you, everyone in my family and to all my friends.

To my coaches, my mentors, teachers, my church United Kingdom International, Pastor Apostle Howard Proctor and to the other churches that I've been a part of, thank you!

I also thank my Prophet and Spiritual Coach, Charles Burch.

I want to give a shout out to my boys, brothers, my heart, 941 All Day Everyday! Thanks to all my sponsors throughout my career and to each of you who always believed in me, too many to name. Thanks to Kanani Kekahuna for helping me put this book together.

A very special Thank You to my Guardian Angel, Gayle Luper.

Finally, I want to thank Pastor Joseph Anthony Schroeder for being my editor and helping me bring this life changing booklet for kids to fruition!

Thank you to USA Fence for sponsoring my boxing gym in Manatee County at The Manatee Police Athletic League/ Team China Smith. I would also like to thank my Guardian Angels for always having my back!

Thank you all so much!
I Love you all,

China "the Dragon" Smith
The People's Champ

Welcome to your new life! Go The Way of the Dragon!

Hi, thanks for taking your time to look at this little book. I wrote it for YOU! Now I know you would rather be hanging out with your friends, but to tell you the truth, I would like to be one of your best friends! That's right; I am Heavy Weight Boxing Champion, China the Dragon Smith. But I'm not bragging about it, I just want you to know, when I was a kid, I was just like you, I didn't think I had much of a chance to achieve any of my dreams. But then, I made a plan to succeed. I call it The Way of the Dragon!

I wrote this because I care about young people; I'm telling you this because I just want to give you a few tips to having your own incredible life! This is a chance at a really cool life. I worked hard to become a Boxing Champion! That's pretty cool, don't you think? What if your life could become even better than mine but maybe in your own way? Do you have dreams and goals? Well some of mine have amazingly come true! Your dreams can come true too!

It's not going to be easy. Anybody can go the easy route and accomplish nothing. It's going be difficult and challenging. There is no way around it. It's all part of the process. It's how you perceive it and act upon it that makes a huge difference. There's probably going to be people that will offend you. Well, you are going to make some people mad too, whether it will be intentional or not. You won't even know, just because you are working towards your goal and dreams. So, get out your feelings, just get that out of your way because I am here for you. The Champ is going to have your back all the way. That is, if you let me!

Each generation of young people is affected by the previous generation. Your parents are in a different generation than you. Then again, your grandparents are in a different generation than you and your parents. You should keep the good parts of their lives that they gave you! But if some things they passed on to you weren't good, then following The Way of the Dragon will change you for the better!

I am going to help you break off the bad ways, and teach you the Way of the Dragon. I want to help you change your mind, just like I changed mine. I'm going to help you step outside the box, just like I did. You can make a big difference in life, and people will admire you for it. The sky's the limit. The only limits we actually have are the limits that we put on ourselves. Sure, I don't expect you to get it all now. But I want to help you take control of your own life, so you can make great choices. I am going to teach you to strategize.

Like me, sometimes you will find great peace to just admit, "I blew it!" But most of the time, you can say "Wow! I did that just because I believed in myself, and I followed the Way of the Dragon!"

I'm going to help you one day at a time. You now have me to lean on, my shoulder to cry on. We together can do this. I truly believe in you and you will start believing in yourself, if you already don't. Crazy as it may sound; there is not that much difference between someone who is successful and someone who is not. A part of you may be weak, even though you don't want to show it, and a part of you may be tough. On one side you might be making dumb mistakes. But in another way you are doing great! It's just a going to take a simple mind change! You believe or you don't believe. I am asking you to believe in yourself because I believe in you!

Get ready now for you to discover,

The Way of the Dragon!

Contents

Introduction   13

Dragon Action One
The Dragon's Wakeup Call   17

Dragon Action Two
Get The Dragon's Courage   21

Dragon Action Three
The Dragon Fights Through   25

Dragon Action Four
Dragons Make No Excuses   29

Dragon Action Five
Dragon Fire–Speaking the Right Words!   35

Dragon Action Six
The Dragon Plans His Actions   41

Dragon Action Seven
Dragons Never Use Their Power to Bully   45
Joseph's Story   47

Final Good Words   55

Introduction

I love to say, "I'm China Smith 24/7," meaning how I act on Sunday morning is the same as I'm going act on Saturday night. I have struggled in my life and failed at lots of things. I also have been very successful. What I have learned is that I have the power to change my circumstances and situations. Now I'm not saying it will be easy and sometimes it seems impossible, but with God all things are possible.

The Process

I wrote this to help you understand that there is greatness inside of you. If you are willing to go through the process for a change. Where do you start? Everything starts from within you. You start by believing in yourself. You are probably saying, "But I don't believe in myself." Well I say, "Maybe not yet, but follow me and your will!"

— China Smith —

Start by looking in the mirror, and repeat this after me.

- I'm somebody special
- I'm a great person
- I believe in myself
- I can do anything I put my mind to
- I love myself, I believe in myself
- I'm a smart person
- I'm needed, I'm an important person
- I'm here for a reason
- I am loved

I need you say these statements above at least 3 times a day and 3 times at a time. Speak it out loud with confidence. See, you maybe feeling rough, bad or down. It's ok we all feel that way at times. But what I need you to do is only speak out loud positive things about yourself. Try this for 30 days and I'm sure your life will change in a better position then before. Thats all we need to get started and make a change. You can do this, I believe in you! I love you.

I can't wait to hear your testimony on how **The Way of the Dragon** helped you change your life. We can and will do this! I will be right here every step of the way.

We have the game plan to enable you to change your life. I'm repeating this because its so important to me and it will be very important to you and you will thank me later. I just want you to win. Stop looking at and blaming other people. You have the power and control within.

Dragon Action
One

The Dragon's Wakeup Call

When you wake up in the morning,
get woke' the Dragon Way!

PRAY!

You say you don't know how to pray?
That's normal because nobody may have taught you.

Well, do you know how to talk to someone that you care about? OK, then just talk to God like you would to anybody else, but talk to Him with respect.

Notice how I capitalize the word 'Him?' We of the Dragon Way do that only for God!

> **Talk to God with:**
> **RESPECT**

> **And talk to Him as:**
> **a FRIEND**

The Sacred Writing says this:

"Our Father in heaven, hallowed be your name. Your kingdom come, your will be done, on earth as it is in heaven. Give us this day our daily bread, and forgive us our debts, as we also have forgiven our debtors. And lead us not into temptation, but deliver us from evil."   Luke 11:2–4 (ESV)

Here is the Sacred Writing decoded:

- God in heaven, I know You are Holy and good.
- I want the plan that You designed for me in heaven to happen here on earth.
- I do need some things from You so I am asking You to help me.
- Please forgive me for the bad stuff I have done, I want to do better.

- I may not feel like it, but I forgive the people who have hurt me.

- Please help me to make the right choice when I am tempted to do wrong.

- Please give me Your POWER to do the right thing every time.

AMEN

The Way of the Dragon starts with a good relationship with God. The Way the Dragon is to start the day in prayer not only for ourselves but for others as well

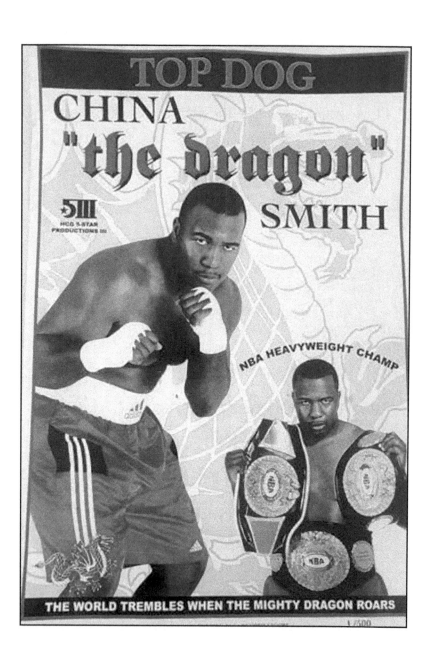

Dragon Action
Two

Get The Dragon's Courage

The word "Courage" means to be brave and to overcome fear. In the jungle the lion is known for its courage. The Dragon is also seen as a creature that is not afraid.

Not everyone is naturally courageous, but when following the Way of the Dragon, everyone can become courageous. Do you know that we can actually help others be full of courage? How do we do that? We do that by encouraging our friends and everyone we meet. To encourage means to put courage into someone by means of positive words and compliments and letting them know that you believe in them.

Parent Dragons need to put courage in to their kids by speaking to them in a way that shows they believe in them and will always be there for them.

Maybe your parents did not do that for you. That said, that does not mean that you cannot have courage. That's why I, heavyweight champion China Smith, wrote *The Way of the Dragon*. I want to encourage you. I want you to encourage your friends. Everyone needs encouragement. Everyone needs courage.

Nobody respects a weak lion or a weak Dragon. Nobody respects a weak person. God loves them but nobody wants to be weak. It would be our job as Dragons to encourage them, so they can be strong too.

The Sacred Writing says this:

The Lord is my light and my salvation, of whom shall, I fear? The Lord is the stronghold of my life of whom shall I be afraid? When the wicked advance against me to devour me, it is my enemies and my foes who will stumble and fall. Though an army besiege me, my heart will not fear; though war breaks out against me, even then, I will be confident. Psalm 27:1-3

Here is the Sacred Writing decoded:

- God shines His light on me and saves me.
- The Lord God gives me strength inside, so I won't be afraid of anything.

- God will see to it that if anyone is against me, they will fail.

- Even if a bunch of people seem to be against me, I will hold onto my confidence in God and in who I am.

- The great thing about life is that you always have choices. The choice is yours. The power lies in your hands. Some things that will happen in your life will be out of your control, but how you deal with it is your choice, so the outcome is totally up to you.

Every action has a consequence!

The Way the Dragon commands that we encourage every person we meet.

Dragon Action
Three

The Dragon Fights Through

Imagine seeing a cool looking tunnel and thinking how much fun it would be to crawl through that tunnel to get to the other side! Let's just say that the tunnel is about 30 feet long and on the other side is an incredible place of fun with your friends. But let's say that after you crawl into the tunnel, you don't feel like going the rest of the way. What would happen? Well, you either need to backup to get out or you're just going to be stuck there. You could even say that you are blocking other kids from their desire to get to the other side because you are in the way! Even if you're tired halfway through, you've got to keep pushing yourself to get to the other side of the tunnel to have fun with your friends.

Life is like that as well. Every day you are required or you desire to start something. There will always be quitters. Quitters quit. Are you a quitter? Then let me help you follow the Way the Dragon. The dragons never quit no matter how hard it is, no matter how long it takes no matter what we have to go through.

We are going to get to the other side in every endeavor. For this to be true, you must be willing to go through the process to get to the other side, that is if you really want to get there.

You being on this earth, and starting to follow the Way of the Dragon is no accident. I don't care what anyone says, it's all part of God's plan. The Way of the Dragon, after all, is THE WAY OF GOD!

The Sacred Writing says this:

Therefore, my beloved brothers, be steadfast and immovable. Always excel in the work of the Lord, because you know that your labor in the Lord is not in vain.   *1 Cor. 15:58*

Here is the Sacred Writing decoded:

To my young Dragons,

- Do not ever give up, humbly yet powerfully, stand your ground.

- Always make sure you are giving the best you got,

- Because you know that all your hard work, will not be wasted, but will be greatly and openly rewarded by God!

The Way of the Dragon is to fight through obstacles and never quit in order to succeed.

Dragon Action
Four

Dragons Make No Excuses

Everyone is born to be successful, but at the same time we are born into different circumstances. Our circumstances are the way things are around us at birth. One child is born into a wealthy family, but his parents always criticize him so he feels like a failure. Another child is born into a poor family but his parents always encourage him so he feels loved and is confident. However, God designed them both to be successful.

Bad circumstances set us up for doubt and distraction in the decisions we make. So we may have adults and friends in our life who were born in bad situations and have doubted themselves. Because of that they did not get the good results of success that they had expected. I'm here to say that other people's experiences, with the circumstances they faced, does not have to be your story.

You have the ability to change, if you prepare yourself for it. Now remember, it may not be easy. Most of the time it's not going to be easy, but very difficult. That is why I am showing you the Way of the Dragon, which is really the way that God has planned for you. If you choose it, if you want it, you can do it. Prepare for it, plan for it and you will get there. You will achieve it.

You must surround yourself with adults and friends that have accomplished some of the things that you are striving for. Get advice from people who have done it because their advice is authentic. Part of the process to your success is not hanging out with all those who have a negative impact on you reaching your goals. If they are not encouraging you, they are discouraging you. Discourage means that they are taking your courage out of you. Be sure to seek people who are solid in their advice and experience. Fill your time with people who also want you to be successful.

You owe it to yourself to make the best of the new day you are given. We are all given the same 24 hours in a day, make them count.

In order for you to work with others, you need to know your identity. Evaluate yourself. Who are you? Where are you at? Are you happy with where you're at? If not, let's work on a better situation. We are all a work in progress. It's okay to make mistakes. Don't allow the mistakes to shape you, learn from them.

Most people never realize it, but IF YOU EVEN WAKE UP IN THE MORNING; you are starting off with a blessing. There will always be a million and one reasons to tell yourself you're not blessed. But the fact that you opened your eyes and you are up and breathing, you are already starting off better than those who didn't wake up to live another day. Even in your lowest and darkest days, you still woke up, so again, you are starting off better than many others. Let's make it count!

Make today be your day! Say, "I'm here. I'm going to own this day. I am going to do things that will make me better in a small way. I am going to make it my goal to encourage someone along the way! My blessing starts out with me waking up to a new day and THAT ALONE MAKES ME GRATEFUL TO GOD, because only He gives me a new day."

No matter how bad it looks or sounds, you can turn your life around. Lots of people may say it's too late for you. Just because they didn't do the hard work to be successful, they want you to stay down. They may not even know that they are doing this. But for you, this is your day that the Lord has made for you, rejoice and glad in it. Again, you are here! Renew your mind and renew your actions.

Now that you know the truth, refuel yourself. Turn away any negativity. Stop looking outward and instead look within yourself for strength. It is there that you will build upon your self-respect and self-confidence.

You, whoever you say you are, no matter what anyone says about you, only you can change and accept who you want and claim to be. Or you can choose not to. It's your decision, you own it. Either way, you are not wrong. Say and speak positive things about yourself, whether or not you feel that way, and you will walk into your destiny.

The Sacred Writing says this:

His lord said unto him, well done, good and faithful servant; thou hast been faithful over a few things, I will make thee ruler over many things: enter thou into the joy of thy Lord. Matt 25:23

Here is the Sacred Writing decoded:

- If you make no excuses, work hard and take responsibility,
- Then God says to you, and your Coach says to you;
- Great job, you are good and diligently following the Way,
- I see that you get small jobs done with excellence and no loose ends,

— The Way of the Dragon —

- So I am going to put you in charge in a lot of different ways in life,
- And I will make you happy to the very end!

The Way of the Dragon is to make no excuses, simply do the right thing. If you fail, admit it, say you are sorry, and get right back on to the Way of the Dragon, because Dragons Fly!

Dragon Action
Five

Dragon Fire – Speaking the Right Words!

Fire is awesome! There is something about fire that draws us close, but at the same time, you can't touch fire. It doesn't matter how strong you are, fire will stop you in your tracks. It doesn't matter how big the obstacle, fire can burn it down. But fire in the Scriptures is used to show the power of God. And fire is a great thing when used in a positive way. The Dragon is known for being undefeatable because of the fire that comes out of his mouth. That fire is invincible and all-powerful against his enemies.

So, in a good way, let's look at the words we speak, just like the fire that comes out of the mouth of the dragon. Your enemy may be that you don't see any way that you can accomplish anything great. Your enemy is your negative thinking because of the circumstances that surround you.

But I have good news for you; you can destroy anything negative that stands in your way with the fire of your word, when your mouth speaks good words.

Your mouth must say what you will do and you cannot change what you say no matter what you face. You believe and you say, "This is what I'm going to do so that I can help others and so that I can live a powerful and good life. I can become everything that God has called me to be. I can be a champion in whatever I choose to do. Not that I'm against anyone else, no I am for everybody else. But only I can direct my life and so I will direct it by saying the right words."

The Way of the Dragons is to speak good words and dragons always speak positively.

Start speaking this way today, it will take some time, but then you will get good at it and you will see that good things start to happen!

No matter what you decide to do, other than this, you will fail unless you speak positive words.

You always speak positive words about other people and you always speak positive words about yourself. This is the *Way of the Dragon*. This is the way to success!

When I was about 9 years old I knew I wanted to be a professional football player or boxer. Words are powerful, I began speaking it at age 9. Nine year later I became that, a professional boxer. I knew nothing about the process I just dreamed of it coming true. All I knew was, I am going to believe and speak that.

People may not have believed it and it was hard to do, but looking back over my life, it's just that simple. It's simple to say something good or bad and watch it happen in your life.

If I had said, "there is no way I can become a professional boxer, because I am poor and a nobody, then I would never have become the Heavyweight Champion. You would never be reading this book because, maybe, I would have just started taking drugs and given up.

So I say to all you little Dragons, be very careful what you speak out of your mouth. Speaking positive words will help you through your obstacles and challenges. We as Dragons can get through the stuff against us. I believe in you. There is Greatness in you. I love you and can't wait to hear your story!

Try This!

- Put your arm out straight in front of you,
- Make a fist, and then point your finger at somebody.
- Look at your hand and you will see only one finger pointing at them

- Look at your thumb; it is over three fingers pointing back at you.

- Never accuse or judge someone else, instead spend three times your effort improving yourself!

The Sacred Writing says this:

Death and life are in the power of the tongue, and they that love it shall eat the fruit thereof.

—Proverbs 18:21

Here is the Sacred Writing decoded:

- The death of your dreams and your life,
- As well as a good and successful life,
- Are totally in your power, in every word you speak.
- They that love to talk will get exactly what they say, whatever it is you say!

The Way of the Dragon is to say good words, to speak good things about yourself without bragging, and to say good things to everyone you meet.

Dragon Action Six

The Dragon Plans His Actions

As each day goes by, you may be acting impulsively, in other words, without thinking. When something negative happens to you, maybe you go on what your feelings are at the moment, instead of waiting a little bit to think before you act. Give yourself time to calm down and think clearly. You see, young dragon, reacting instantly seems to be the normal thing to do, but it is NOT the Way of the Dragon!

I want to teach you to focus on you and bettering yourself. You have no competition other than what you create or tell yourself in your mind. Focusing on you and working on a better you is a job all by itself. I'm not saying you should be self-secluded all the time. If you need to take some time for yourself to rejuvenate, then, by all means go right ahead. It's helpful for you and the people around you.

Start now and take the right steps toward your goals and vision so that you are ready and prepared as you can be at your age, and even more prepared as you get older. Trust me you will thank me later. If there is something good that you want, go get it! Think it through and get a strategy and a game plan to do it the right way. It is always good to get advice from successful people. Never ask advice from someone worse off than you, someone who is not trying to achieve goals.

Trusting a person older than you, who is doing well, will help you. If you listen to or follow those people who are succeeding, that will be better compared to the ones that make bad mistakes over and over again and struggle all the time.

I am saying watch how achievers plan, how they have a goal and how they take action. The great thing is my young dragon, today you can become a Champion Boxer's friend, that's me and I want to be your friend and help you. You are not doing this all on your own. We are a team, and you are getting better every day by doing things the Dragon's way. The choice is yours!

The Sacred Writing says this:

A man's mind plans his way, but the Lord directs his steps and makes them sure. —*Proverbs 16:9*

Here is the Sacred Writing decoded:

- A young man should make a plan and follow it as best he can,

- God will be pleased with this, so God will direct him even better than his own plan,

- And make him feel secure and correct in the young man's decisions.

The Way of the Dragon is to stop and think before you act, get good advice, make a simple plan to achieve your goal and take action, one step and one day at a time!

Dragon Action
Seven

Dragons Never Use Their Power to Bully

We all know what a bully is, it's one of the worst things that you can be. A person who bullies is actually a person who is trying to show you, and everyone else, that they are superior to you and everybody else. Because they are bigger, they are selfish, and they think people will admire them because they always win. That is the worst kind of pride and it will backfire on them. One day they will meet somebody that is stronger than them and they will be humiliated in front of everyone. Now they have nothing to be admired about them and everybody will see right through them. Because they are bigger, they are selfish, and they think people will admire them because they always win.

Well, the truth is bullies are weak inside, they are very weak and the only way they feel that they can get any self-esteem is to pick on people who are usually smaller than them. Bullies don't usually pick a fight with someone that is bigger. Let me make it clear, being a bully is the exact opposite of the Way of the Dragon. Now I am a champion boxer, but that's not bullying, that's a sport. The good boxer respects his opponent and follows the rules. There should be no personal anger at the other boxer. You even try to knock him out, but you never want to hurt him permanently. It's a contest. It is the total opposite of what a bully does. The bully does not respect the person he is picking on, he just wants to inflict harm and humiliation on his victim and that makes him feel good. That is very sad.

So my young Dragons, never let bullying go on in front of you, do whatever you can to stand up to bullies.

Even if you are being bullied, you can overcome it and be successful by following The Way of the Dragon, that's what my friend Joseph did. This is just a little bit of his story. Let's learn from him:

— The Way of the Dragon —

Joseph's Story

*"Hi, my name is Joseph. When I was a little boy, my growth slowed way down. When I was eight years old and my little brother Tony was four years old he was already taller than me. A lot of kids and even grown-ups made fun of me. They called me names like **shrimp, midget, dwarf, half-pint** and **shortie** and they called me names in front of the other kids which further embarrassed me. I started to get overweight and now they also called me names like **fatso** and it really hurt me.*

As I got older and into my teen years, my doctor told me that I was not going to grow anymore. I was 4 feet 11, about the

Little Joseph and his sister, Kathy, are ring bearer and flower girl at a relative's wedding. Kathy is two years younger but already taller than Joseph.

size of a 10-year-old boy. And yet I was 18 years old. It was horrible news, I would have only one life to live and I would always be a tiny man. I happen to be a white person. Think about it, is it better to be a tall black person or a tiny white person for life? What would you choose?

So, back when I was young I would hear people make fun of black people or Jewish people or people with a big nose or people who looked unusual. It made me mad because these were my friends and I told them not to make fun of black people and other people. You see, because I was small I understood what it was like to be bullied and made fun of.

One day I was coming home from my computer technology school in Chicago. I was 19 years old wearing a nice sport coat and tie, carrying a briefcase and a bunch of books under my arm. As I walked along the sidewalk, I could see three black men sitting on the steps of the building that I had to pass by. I was about to say "Hello" but as soon as I got near the three black men, they started to bully me with their words. They said something like this, "Look at the little white boy all dressed up in his cute little suit." They taunted me and laughed at me and mocked me.

I felt so bad and I thought about all the times that I stood up to my friends and told him that black people were just as good as us and other people. That day I found out that you are not good because you are black and you are not good because you are brown and you are not good because you are white or red or yellow. Bad people, and bullies, come in all colors and good people and kind people come in all colors.

I also got physically beat up a number of times as a kid and teenager, one time swelling my face to almost twice the size. But did I let all this stop me in life? No, it was not easy and sometimes I felt like giving up, but I still followed my dreams.

You see, I followed the principles in the Scriptures and I knew God loved me and I had parents that loved me and without even knowing it, I was following The Way of the Dragon! Well, eventually, after many years of hard work, I became Supervisor of IT Operations for large company in Chicago, my home town. I managed three shifts of workers, hiring and firing and

Joseph believed in God, despite his small stature and almost daily bullying, he developed confidence in himself. As told in his story, here he is as Supervisor of Computer Operations. He was the smallest person but was manager over 24 employees. He is standing between two of his men.

training, in the operation of a multimillion dollar computer center! Can you believe it, a 4 foot 11 inch man supervising 6 foot tall men? I was polite but firm and led the way.

After many years I left there and moved to Florida not knowing anybody. I went to Bible school and got married to a wonderful woman, and eventually became a Senior Pastor of a church in Englewood, FL. Then I left there and became the Executive Pastor of a large church in Palmetto, Florida. Finally I became the Campus Pastor in one of the most beautiful churches ever built in Sarasota, Florida. During this time I was elected many times as the President of two ministerial associations.

Yes, I did all this, with the help of God, as a 4 foot 11 inch man who was once bullied and beaten up.

I have been happily married now to my beautiful wife, Lorraine, for 33 years, and we have four kids and 9 grandchildren!

I have traveled to many countries teaching the Bible and also enjoying their culture. I visited Canada and Mexico. I have traveled to Israel and to Spain and Italy. Many times I risked my life preaching the gospel in the dangerous country of Pakistan. Through it all, God was with me.

I am not bragging, I'm just telling you that if you are a young person who is being bullied or does not feel very good about yourself you can accomplish anything you put your mind to, just like world champ China the Dragon Smith and just like the things I've accomplished. Thank you for letting me tell you my story of overcoming bullying by following the principles in the Way of the Dragon.

I am Joseph Anthony Schroeder, author of "My Little Miracle Story." *Thank you for letting me tell my story.*

Yes, I am still 4 foot 11 inches tall!

When Joseph was in his early 30's, he studied the Bible and Ministry. He eventually became a Senior Pastor and Missionary. Here he is in one of the most dangerous countries in the world, Pakistan, with his wife, Lorraine. Standing between them is their security guard with his rifle to protect them from attackers.

Today I am a Writing Coach and I am the contributing editor to the book that you now hold in your hands. With God all things are possible!

Wow, this is China Smith again, wasn't that an incredible story? It is an example for you to follow when you are put down or made fun of, believe in yourself and know that no dream is impossible with God!

The Sacred Writing says this:

Do not act out of selfish ambition or conceit, but with humility think of others as being better than yourselves. —Phil 2:3

Here is the Sacred Writing decoded:

Don't act like you are so important in life and that everything revolves around you. It is true that you are valuable and important to God, but so is the other person. So be a little humble and take the time to treat them like they are someone special, even better than you. It will make them feel good and will make you feel even better inside.

The Way of the Dragon is to never bully anyone. We stand up to bullies and protect our friends. We try to help the bully to come along with us and instead follow The Way of the Dragon. This is a NO BULLY ZONE!

Let Me Give You Some Final Good Words

Well, young dragons, this is going to be an exciting journey that we travel together! We will help each other along the way!

I want you to know, The Way of the Dragon is really the way that Jesus Christ, the Son of God, taught us to live. The sacred writings are the scriptures that are found in the Bible.

Jesus said, "I am the Way, I am the Truth and I am the Life, nobody gets to see God the Father in heaven, except through Me."

So, the Way of the Dragon that I teach in this book is The Way taught to us by Jesus Christ, and only He should get all the Glory! I am His servant.

It is Jesus who helped me become a Heavyweight Champion Boxer; He alone gave me the power. First I asked Him to forgive me of all my sins and give me a fresh start. At that time I prayed a simple prayer like this and I hope you will pray it too:

"Dear God, thank You for sending
Your Son Jesus Christ into this world
to die on the cross for me.
I ask You to forgive me of all my sins
and show me the right way to live.
I accept You as my personal savior
and I ask You fill me with Your
Holy Spirit power so that I can
live a good life.
Please show me how I can
always help others.
Amen"

— China Smith —

— The Way of the Dragon —

— China Smith —

— The Way of the Dragon —

CPSIA information can be obtained
at www.ICGtesting.com
Printed in the USA
BVHW070306260719
554335BV00002B/221/P